The Strength of Fields

CHILDREN'S POETRY

Tucky the Hunter

CRITICISM

Sorties
The Suspect in Poetry
Babel to Byzantium

BELLES-LETTRES

Self-Interviews

JAMES DICKEY

The Strength of Fields

DOUBLEDAY & COMPANY, INC.
GARDEN CITY, NEW YORK

The title poem, "The Strength of Fields," originally appeared in 1977 in a book called *A New Spirit, a New Commitment, a New America*, by the 1977 Inaugural Committee, published by Bantam Books. Copyright © 1977 by James Dickey.

"I Dreamed I Already Loved You," "Assignation," and "Doing the Twist on Nails," translated by James Dickey, are all from *Stolen Apples*, by Yevgeny Yevtushenko. Translation copyright © 1971 by Doubleday & Company, Inc. Reprinted by permission of the publisher.

Some of the other poems in this volume appeared originally in the following publications: "False Youth: Autumn: Clothes of the Age" (issue of November 1971), "Reunioning Dialogue" (issue of January 1973), and "Exchanges" (issue of September 1970) in *The Atlantic*; "For the Death of Lombardi" in *Esquire*, © 1971 by Esquire, Inc.; "Haunting the Maneuvers," copyright © 1969 by Harper's Magazine, reprinted from the January 1970 issue by permission of *Harper's*; "The Voyage of the Needle" (1978 winter issue) in *Gentlemen's Quarterly*; "The Rain Guitar" (January 8, 1972), "Drums Where I Live" (November 26, 1969), "Root-light, or the Lawyer's Daughter" (November 8, 1969), and "Remnant Water" (March 10, 1973) in *The New Yorker*; "Camden Town" in the 1970 spring issue (Vol. 46, No. 2) of *The Virginia Quarterly*.

"Purgation," "The Ax-God: Sea-Pursuit," "Nameless," "Math," "Judas," "Small Song," "Undersea Fragment in Colons," "Mexican Valley," "Low Voice, Out Loud," "Poem," "When," and "A Saying of Farewell" originally appeared in *Head-Deep in Strange Sounds: Free-Flight Improvisations from the unEnglish*, by James Dickey, published by Paleamon Press, Ltd. Copyright © 1979 by James Dickey. Reprinted by permission of the publisher.

ISBN: 0-385-15809-2
Library of Congress Catalog Card Number 79-3034
Copyright © 1979 by James Dickey
All Rights Reserved
Printed in the United States of America

9 8 7 6 5 4 3

To Deborah

in the new life

Contents

HEAD-DEEP IN STRANGE SOUNDS:
FREE-FLIGHT IMPROVISATIONS FROM THE UNENGLISH

The Strength of Fields

Root-light, or the Lawyer's Daughter

That any just to long for
The rest of my life, would come, diving like a lifetime
Explosion in the juices
Of palmettoes flowing
Red in the St. Mary's River as it sets in the east
Georgia from Florida off, makes whatever child
I was lie still, dividing
Swampy states   watching
The lawyer's daughter shocked
With silver   and I wished for all holds
On her like root-light. She came flying
Down from Eugene Talmadge
Bridge, just to long for as I burst with never
Rising never
Having seen her except where she worked
For J. C. Penney in Folkston. Her regular hours
Took fire, and God's burning bush of the morning
Sermon was put on her; I had never seen it where
It has to be. If you asked me how to find the Image

Of Woman to last
All your life, I'd say go lie
Down underwater for nothing
Under a bridge and hold Georgia
And Florida from getting at each other   hold
Like walls of wine. Be eight years old from Folkston ten
From Kingsland twelve miles in the clean palmetto color
Just as it blasts
Down with a body   red and silver buck
Naked with bubbles on Sunday   root
light explodes
Head-down, and there she is.

The Strength of Fields

> *. . . a separation from the world,*
> *a penetration to some source of power*
> *and a life-enhancing return . . .*
> Van Gennep: *Rites de Passage*

Moth-force a small town always has,

Given the night.

What field-forms can be,
Outlying the small civic light-decisions over
A man walking near home?
Men are not where he is
Exactly now, but they are around him   around him like the strength

Of fields.   The solar system floats on
Above him in town-moths.

Tell me, train-sound,

With all your long-lost grief,

what I can give.

Dear Lord of all the fields
                              what am I going to *do?*
                    Street-lights, blue-force and frail
As the homes of men, tell me how to do it   how
     To withdraw   how to penetrate and find the source
          Of the power you always had
                                        light as a moth, and rising
          With the level and moonlit expansion
Of the fields around, and the sleep of hoping men.

     You?   I?   What difference is there?   We can all be saved

          By a secret blooming. Now as I walk
The night   and you walk with me   we know simplicity
     Is close to the source that sleeping men
          Search for in their home-deep beds.

     We know that the sun is away   we know that the sun can be conquered
     By moths, in blue home-town air.
          The stars splinter, pointed and wild. The dead lie under
The pastures.   They look on and help.   Tell me, freight-train,
               When there is no one else
To hear.   Tell me in a voice the sea

Would have, if it had not a better one: as it lifts,
    Hundreds of miles away, its fumbling, deep-structured roar
       Like the profound, unstoppable craving
    Of nations for their wish.
                         Hunger, time and the moon:

The moon lying on the brain
                        as on the excited sea   as on
    The strength of fields.   Lord, let me shake

With purpose. Wild hope can always spring
From tended strength.   Everything is in that.
    That and nothing but kindness.   More kindness, dear Lord
Of the renewing green.
              That is where it all has to start:
With the simplest things. More kindness will do nothing less
    Than save every sleeping one
    And night-walking one

Of us.
    My life belongs to the world. I will do what I can.

Two Poems of the Military

I. Haunting the Maneuvers

Prepared for death and unprepared
For war, there was Louisiana   there was Eisenhower a Lieutenant
Colonel and there was I
As an Invasion Force.   The Defenders were attacking
And I was in the pinestraw
Advancing   inching through the aircraft of the Home
Force.   Sacks of flour were bursting
All over the trees. Now if one of them damned things hits you in the head
It's gonna kill you just as sure as if
It was a real bomb
So watch it.   Yes Sir.   I was watching
It.   One sack came tumbling after
Me no matter
What.   Not in the head,   though,
I thought thank God at least
Not dead.
But I was dead.   The sergeant said go sit
Over there: you are the first man killed.   It's KP for you

For the whole rest of the war.   This war,
Anyway.   Yes Sir.   The Defenders had struck
The first blow: I was plastered.   I thought why this
Is easy: there's not a drop
Of blood there's only death
White on me;   I can live
Through.
I lived through in the Hell
Of latrine duty, but mostly on KP, on metal
Trays that dovetailed to each other, stacked by the ton in the field
Kitchens.   I moved them all at one time
Or other, and the Defenders
Ate   ate and went back to killing
My buddies with blanks and bread.   But when I slept on that well
Defended ground   the pinestraw stirred   each needle pointed up
Into the dark like a compass, and white   whiter
Than my skin, edible, human-eyed through the pines,
Issued a great mass
Laugh   a great lecture-laugh by the chaplain's one
Dirty joke, I rose
Over the unprepared boys   over the war
Games the war

Within a war   over the trucks with mystical signs
On them that said TANK   over World War One
Enfield rifles filled with dud rounds   self-rising
Through the branches   driven up like a small cloud
Of the enemy's food   at the same time bread

And bomb, swanned out like a diver, I came
From my death over both sleeping armies,
Over Eisenhower dreaming of invasion.   Where are you,
My enemy?   My body won't work any more
For you: I stare down like stars
Of yeast: you will have to catch me
And eat me.   Where are you, invading
Friends?   Who else is dead?   O those who are in this
With me, I can see nothing
But what is coming   can say
Nothing but what the first-killed
Working hard all day for his vision
Of war says best: the age-old Why
In God's name Why
In Louisiana, Boys   O Why
In Hell are we doing this?

II. Drums Where I Live

So that sleeping and waking
Drum, drum, every day the first part of the sun,
Its upper rim
And rhythm, I live here. I and my family pass, in the new house,
Into the great light mumbling one
Two three four, marching in place like boys
Laid out, all voices of the living and the dead
To come and hovering
Between brought in
to cadence. It is not
A heart, but many men. Someone said it is
Comfort, comforting to hear them. Not every
Sun-up, neighbor: now and then I wish I had a chance
To take my chances
With silence. More and more
They seem to be waiting
For the day   more and more as my son sighs all over the house
Intercom. I know, I know: he is counting
His years. When we rise, the drums

21

Have stopped. But I know from the jungle of childhood
Movies what that means. There is nothing in the grenades'
Coming-closer bursts to worry
Anyone; they are Expanding
The Range. It is only in the morning
Paper that a trainee hangs himself
On the obstacle course. And it is nothing but nerves
That make something human, a cry,
Float like a needle on the sunlight
From the stockade. But every night I sleep assured
That the drums are going
To reach me at dawn like light
Where I live, and my heart, my blood and my family will assemble
Four barely-livable counts. Dismissed,
Personnel. The sun is clear
Of Basic Training. This time, thís
Is my war and where in God's
Name did it start? In peace, two, three, four:
In peace peace peace peace

One two

In sleep.

The Voyage of the Needle

The child comes sometimes with his mother's needle
And draws a bath with his hand. These are your fifty years
        Of fingers, cast down among
        The hard-driven echoes of tile
In the thresholding sound of run water. Here the sun divides light
        From the Venetian sector of the dark
Where you sink through both,
                and warmly, more slowly than being
Smoothed and stretched, your bodying barge-ripples die.
        A gauze of thin paper upholds
      The needle, then soaks like an eyelid
      And falls, uncontrolling, away.
               The hung metal voyages alone,
     Like the trembling north-nerve of a compass,
On surface tension, that magic, like a mother's spell
Cast in sharp seed in your childhood, in scientific trickery rooted
And flowering in elation. It is her brimming otherworld
That rides on the needle's frail lake, on death's precarious membrane,
     Navigating through all slanted latitudes,

Containing a human body
She gave, and saved to bear, by a spell
From physics, this fragile cargo. "Mother," you say,
"I am lying in a transference
Of joy and glory: come to me
From underground, from under the perilous balance
Of a thicket of thorns. I lie
As unmoving. Bring the needle to breathless harbor
Somewhere on my body, that I may rise
And tell. My sex is too deep,
My eyes too high for your touch. O let it reach me at the lips'
Water-level, the thorns burst
Into rain on your wooded grave, the needle plunge
Through the skin of charmed water and die, that I may speak at last
With up-bearing magic
Of this household, weightless as love."

The Rain Guitar

—England, 1962—

The water-grass under had never waved
But one way.   It showed me that flow is forever
Sealed from rain in a weir.   For some reason having
To do with Winchester, I was sitting on my guitar case
Watching nothing but eelgrass trying to go downstream with all the right motions
But one.   I had on a sweater, and my threads were opening
Like mouths with rain.   It mattered to me not at all
That a bridge was stumping
With a man, or that he came near and cast a fish
thread into the weir.   I had no line and no feeling.
I had nothing to do with fish
But my eyes on the grass they hid in, waving with the one move of trying
To be somewhere else.   With what I had, what could I do?
I got out my guitar, that somebody told me was supposed to improve
With moisture—or was it when it dried out?—and hit the lowest
And loudest chord.   The drops that were falling just then

Hammered like Georgia railroad track
With E.   The man went into a kind of fishing
Turn.   Play it, he said through his pipe.   There
I went, fast as I could with cold fingers.   The strings shook
With drops.   A buck dance settled on the weir.   Where was the city
Cathedral in all this?   Out of sight, but somewhere around.
Play a little more
Of that, he said, and cast.   Music-wood shone,
Getting worse or better faster than it liked:
Improvement or disintegration
Supposed to take years, fell on it
By the gallon.   It darkened and rang
Like chimes. My sweater collapsed, and the rain reached
My underwear.   I picked, the guitar showered, and he cast to the mountain
Music.   His wood leg tapped
On the cobbles.   Memories of many men
Hung, rain-faced, improving, sealed-off
In the weir.   I found myself playing Australian
Versions of British marching songs.   Mouths opened all over me; I sang,
His legs beat and marched
Like companions.   I was Air Force,
I said.   So was I; I picked

This up in Burma, he said, tapping his gone leg
With his fly rod, as Burma and the South
west Pacific and North Georgia reeled,
Rapped, cast, chimed, darkened and drew down
Cathedral water, and improved.

Remnant Water

Here in the thrust-green

Grass-wind and thin surface now nearly
Again and again for the instant

Each other   hair-lined backwater barely there and it
Utterly:
this that was deep flashing—
Tiny grid-like waves   wire-touched water—
No more, and comes what is left

Of the gone depths duly arriving
Into the weeds belly-up:
one carp now knowing grass
And also thorn-shucks and seeds
Can outstay him:
next to the slain lake the inlet
Trembles   seine-pressure in something of the last
Rippling   grass in the slow-burning

Slow-browning dance learned from green;

A hundred acres of canceled water come down
To death-mud shaking
Its one pool   stomach-pool   holding the dead one diving up
Busting his gut in weeds   in scum-gruel glowing with belly-white
Unhooked   around him all grass in a bristling sail taking off back-
blowing. Here in the dry hood I am watching
Alone, in my tribal sweat   my people gone my fish rolling
Beneath me   and I die
Waiting   will wait out
The blank judgment given only
In ruination's suck-holing acre   wait and make the sound surrounding NO

Laugh primally: be
Like an open-gut flash   an open under-
water eye with the thumb
pressure to brain the winter-wool head of me,
Spinning my guts with my fish in the old place,
Suffering its consequences, dying,
Living up to it.

Two Poems of Flight-Sleep

I. Camden Town

—Army Air Corps,
Flight Training, 1943—

With this you trim it. Do it right and the thing'll fly
Itself. Now get up there and get those lazy-
eights down.   A check-ride's coming at you
Next week.
                          I took off in the Stearman like stealing two hundred and twenty horses
Of escape from the Air Corps.
                                        The cold turned purple with the open
Cockpit, and the water behind me being
The East, dimmed out. I put the nose on the white sun
And trimmed the ship. The altimeter made me
At six thousand feet. We were stable: myself, the plane,
                          The earth everywhere

Small in its things with cold
But vast beneath.   The needles on the panel
All locked together, and a banner like World War One
Tore at my head, streaming from my helmet in the wind.
I drew it down   down under the instruments
Down where the rudder pedals made small corrections
Better than my feet   down where I could ride on faith
And trim, the aircraft slightly cocked
But holding the West by a needle.   I was in
Death's baby machine, that led to the fighters and bombers,
But training, here in the lone purple,
For something else.   I pulled down my helmet-flaps and droned
With flight-sleep.   Near death
My watch stopped.   I knew it, for I felt the Cadet
Barracks of Camden die like time, and "There's a war on"
Die, and no one could groan from the dark of the bottom
Bunk to his haggard instructor, I tried
I tried to do what you said   I tried   tried
No;   never.   No one ever lived to prove he thought he saw
An aircraft with no pilot showing: I would have to become
A legend, curled up out of sight with all the Western World
Coming at me under the floor-mat, minute after minute, cold azures,

Small trains and warbound highways,
All entering flight-sleep.   Nothing mattered but to rest in the winter
Sun beginning to go
Down early.   My hands in my armpits, I lay with my sheep-lined head
Next to the small air-moves
Of the rudder pedals, dreaming of letting go   letting go
The cold   the war   the Cadet Program and my peanut-faced
Instructor and his maps. No maps   no world   no love
But this.   Nothing can fail when you go below
The instruments.   Wait till the moon.   Then.   Then.
But no.   When the waters of Camden Town died, then so
Did I, for good.   I got up bitterly, bitter to be
Controlling, re-entering the fast colds
Of my scarf, and put my hands and feet where the plane was made
For them.   My goggles blazed with darkness as I turned,
And the compass was wrenched from its dream
Of all the West.   From luxurious
Death in uncaring I swung
East, and the deaths and nightmares
And training of many.

II.   Reunioning Dialogue

—*New York, 1972,*
St. Moritz bar—

Didn't we double!
                    Sure, when we used to lie out under the wing
               Double-teaming the Nips near our own hole
                    In the ground   opening an eye

For the Southern Cross, and we'd see something cut the stars

Out into some kind of shape, the shape of a new Widow

Black Widow
                    and all over the perimeter the ninety millimeters would open

               Up on Heaven   the sirens would go off
               And we'd know better than not to dive
                                        for the palm logs,
          The foxhole filled with fear-slime, and lie there,
     Brains beating like wings
                    our new wings from Northrop,   33

The enemy looking for the aircraft
We slept under.
                          Well, we knew what we wanted,
        Didn't we?
                      To get out from under our own wings,
        To let them lift us
                            together
                                      lift us out of the sleep
With a hole in it, and slot back fresh windows and climb in the squared-off   cool
        Of the Cross.
                          Angels, Observer!
                                      Nine thousand angels,
            Pilot!   The altitude of the Heavenly Host

        In the Philippines is that completely air-conditioned
    Nine thousand feet!
                          I couldn't wait to fool with the automatic pilot,

        And I went absolutely crazy over Howard Hughes' last word
        In radar!
                          Remember?
                                      We were pulling convoy cover.
        By my figures we were seven hundred miles south of base, my eyes brilliant sweeps

Of electronic yellow, watching the spinner painting-in the fleet,
The arranged, lingering images of the huge fortunes
Of war   the great distances and secret relationships
Between tankers and troopships   and on my screen, God's small, brilliant chess-set
Of world war, as we sat

Circling

relaxing in all the original freshness
Of the Cross, comfortable and light
And deadly: night-cool of nine thousand angels
Over the fleet.

You called back with clear, new
Electricity: Hey, Buddy, how're you liking this?
What a war! I said. The scope just pulses away
Like a little old yellow heart. The convoy comes in, the convoy goes out
And comes right back in for you and me
And Uncle Sam.

It was easy,
Right? Milk run? Why, by God, we *flew* on milk!
I cut-in the automatic pilot and leaned back
In the cool of those southern stars, and could have spent the rest of my life
Watching the gyros jiggle the wheel
With little moves like an invisible man   like a ghost
Was flying us. The next thing I knew the intercom busted in   35

With YOU   I looked down and out

I looked the radar down
To the depths of its empty yellow heart. *I didn't have a ship*
To my name.

And I said where in Hell
Are we?   Jesus God, I was afraid of my watch   afraid to look
Afraid the son of a bitch had stopped. But no,
Four hours had gone to Hell
Somewhere in the South Pacific. Our engines were sucking wind,
Running on fumes, and I started calling everything that had a code
Name south of our island. Nothing.   but I thought of the five boys
From our squadron   all volleyball players
With no heads, and all but one
Island south of us was Japanese. I thought I could hear the sword swish,
But it was a wisp arriving
In my earphones   an American spirit crackling
That we were over Cebu. They had one strip and no lights,
Lumps and holes in the runway and the moon
Almost gone. I said to the Seabees get me a couple of things
That burn; I'll try to come down between 'em.

—Can you hold out for fifteen minutes?—

Just about.

They doubled. Two pairs of lights came running.
Together   then split   stopped and gave us five thousand devilish feet
Of blackness laid out maybe on the ground. I said hold on,
Buddy; this may just be it. We drifted in   full
Flaps   nose-high   easing   easing   cleared the first lighted jeep

Hit and

Bounced   came down again hit a hole
And double-bounced   the great new night-
gathering binoculars came unshipped and banged me in the head
As I fought for hot, heavy ground,
Trying to go straight for the rest of my life
For the other jeep,
Doing anything and everything to slaughter
The speed, and finally down
Got down to the speed of a jeep   down
Down and turned off into the bushes that'd been pouring
By   pouring with sweat and killed
The engine. Man, was I shaking! I couldn't even undo the hatch.
You pounded at me
From underneath. I'm all right, I said, drawing in the stuffed heat of life,
Of my life. I climbed down, rattling the new black
California bolts of the wings.

Buddy, would you sit there and tell me,
How we got over Cebu? Why, it was the wrong goddamned *island!*
Why didn't you give me a course
Correction? Our million dollar Black Widow bird like to've carried us off
And killed us! How come you didn't say a thing
For four hours?

I'm sorry, Pilot, but that Southern Cross
Had the most delicious lungs
For me. We'd jumped out of our hole
On wings   the heat was off   and weight, and I could breathe
At last. I was asleep.

Well, for the Lord's sake,
Observer   Navigator   Miracle
Map-reader   second half of the best
Two-man crew in night-fighters, as we sit here
In Central Park, where on earth in that war
Have we *been?*

I don't know. I told you I was asleep.

Well, Old Buddy, the ghosts had us
For sure, then. Ghosts and angels. Nobody else.
I guess   in Central Park   I can tell you, too, after all
These years. So was I.

For the Death of Lombardi

I never played for you. You'd have thrown
Me off the team on my best day—
No guts, maybe not enough speed,
Yet running in my mind
As Paul Hornung, I made it here
With the others, sprinting down railroad tracks,
Hurdling bushes and backyard Cyclone
Fences, through city after city, to stand, at last, around you
Exhausted, exalted, pale
As though you'd said "Nice going": pale
As a hospital wall. You are holding us
Millions together: those who played for you, and those who entered the bodies
Of Bart Starr, Donny Anderson, Ray Nitchke, Jerry Kramer
Through the snowing tube on Sunday afternoon,
Warm, playing painlessly
In the snows of Green Bay Stadium, some of us drunk
On much-advertised beer   some old   some in other
Hospitals—most, middle-aged
And at home. Here you summon us, lying under

The surgical snows.   Coach, look up: we are here:
We are held in this room
Like cancer.
The Crab has you, and to him
And to us you whisper
Drive, *Drive.*   Jerry Kramer's face floats near—real, pale—
We others dream ourselves
Around you, and far away in the mountains, driving hard
Through the drifts, Marshall of the Vikings, plunging   burning
Twenty-dollar bills to stay alive, says, still
Alive, "I wouldn't be here
If it weren't for the lessons of football."   Vince, they've told us:
When the surgeons got themselves
Together and cut loose
Two feet of your large intestine, the Crab whirled up   whirled out
Of the lost gut and caught you again
Higher up.   Everyone's helpless
But cancer.   Around your bed the knocked-out teeth like hail-pebbles
Rattle down   miles of adhesive tape from hands and ankles
Writhe in the room like vines   gallons of sweat blaze in buckets
In the corners   the blue and yellow of bruises

Make one vast sunset around you.   No one understands you.

Coach, don't you know that some of us were ruined
For life?   Everybody can't win.   What of almost all
Of us, Vince?   We lost.   And our greatest loss was that we could not survive
Football.   Paul Hornung has withdrawn
From me, and I am middle-aged and gray, like these others.
What holds us here?   It is that you are dying by the code you made us
What we are by.   Yes, Coach, it is true: love-hate is stronger
Than either love or hate.   Into the weekly, inescapable dance
Of speed, deception, and pain
You led us, and brought us here weeping.
But as men.   Or, you who created us as George
Patton created armies, did you discover the worst
In us: aggression   meanness   deception   delight in giving
Pain to others, for money?   Did you make of us, indeed,
Figments   over-specialized, brutal ghosts
Who could have been real
Men in a better sense?   Have you driven us mad
Over nothing?   Does your death set us free?

Too late.   We stand here among
Discarded TV commercials:
Among beer-cans and razor-blades and hair-tonic bottles,

Stinking with male deodorants: we stand here
Among teeth and filthy miles
Of unwound tapes, novocaine needles, contracts, champagne
Mixed with shower-water, unraveling elastic, bloody faceguards,
And the Crab, in his new, high position
Works soundlessly. In dying
You give us no choice, Coach,
Either. We've got to believe there's such a thing
As winning. The Sunday spirit-screen
Comes on   the bruise-colors brighten   deepen
On the wall   the last tooth spits itself free
Of a line-backer's aging head   knee-cartilage cracks,
A boy wraps his face in a red jersey and crams it into
A rusty locker to sob, and we're with you
We're with you all the way
You're going forever, Vince.

False Youth: Autumn: Clothes of the Age

—for Susan Tuckerman Dickey—

Three red foxes on my head, come down
There last Christmas from Brooks Brothers
As a joke, I wander down Harden Street
In Columbia, South Carolina, fur-haired and bald,
Looking for impulse in camera stores and redneck greeting cards.
A pole is spinning
Colors I have little use for, but I go in
Anyway, and take off my fox hat and jacket
They have not seen from behind yet. The barber does what he can
With what I have left, and I hear the end man say, as my own
Hair-cutter turns my face
To the floor, Jesus, if there's anything I hate
It's a middle-aged hippie. Well, so do I, I swallow
Back: so do I   so do I
And to hell. I get up, and somebody else says
When're you gonna put on that hat,

Buddy? Right now. Another says softly,
        Goodbye, Fox. I arm my denim jacket
On and walk to the door, stopping for the murmur of chairs,
And there it is
                          hand-stitched by the needles of the mother
Of my grandson   ·eagle riding on his claws with a banner
        Outstretched as the wings of my shoulders,
                Coming after me with his flag
                Disintegrating, his one eye raveling
                Out, filthy strings flying
        From the white feathers, one wing nearly gone:
                Blind eagle but flying
        Where I walk, where I stop with my fox
Head at the glass to let the row of chairs spell it out
        And get a lifetime look at my bird's
One word, raggedly blazing with extinction and soaring loose
In red threads burning up white until I am shot in the back
        Through my wings   or ripped apart
                For rags:

Poetry.

For the Running of the New York City Marathon

If you would run

If you would quicken the city with your pelting,
Then line up, be counted, and change
Your body into time, and with me through the boxed maze flee
On soft hooves, saying   all saying in flock-breath
Take me there.

I am against you
And with you: I am second
Wind and native muscle in the streets   my image lost and discovered
Among yours: lost and found in the endless panes
Of a many-gestured bald-headed woman, caught between
One set of clothes and tomorrow's: naked, pleading in her wax
For the right, silent words to praise
The herd-hammering pulse of our sneakers,
And the time gone by when we paced
River-sided, close-packed in our jostled beginning,
O my multitudes.

We are streaming from the many to the one   45

At a time, our ghosts chopped-up by the windows
Of merchants; the mirroring store-fronts let us, this one day,
Wear on our heads feet and backs
What we would wish. This day I have taken in my stride
Swank jogging-suits rayed with bright emblems
Too good for me: have worn in blood-sweating weather
Blizzard-blind parkas and mukluks, a lightning-struck hairpiece
Or two, and the plumes of displayed Zulu chieftains.

Through the colors of day I move as one must move
His shadow somewhere on
Farther into the dark. Any hour now   any minute
Attend the last rites
Of pure plod-balance! Smoke of the sacrificial
Olympic lamb in the Deli! O swooping and hairline-hanging
Civic-minded placement of bridges! Hallelujas of bars!
Teach those who have trained in the sunrise
On junk-food and pop, how to rest   how to rise
From the timed city's never-die dead. Through the spattering echo
Of Vulcanized hundreds, being given the finish-line hot-foot,
I am lolloping through to the end,
By man-dressing mannequins clad   by flashes of sun on squared rivers

As we breast our own breathless arrival: as we home in,
                    Ahead of me   me   and behind me
All winning over the squirrel-wheel's outlasted stillness, on the unearthly pull and fall
                    Of our half-baked soles, all agony-
                    smiles and all winning—

                    All winning, one after one.

Exchanges

(Phi Beta Kappa Poem, Harvard, 1970)

*—being in the form of a dead-living dialogue with
Joseph Trumbull Stickney (1874—1904)—*

(Stickney's words are in italics)

Under the cliff, green powered in from the open,
Changed   and she
And I crouched at the edge
Five hundred feet above the ocean's suicide in a horizon
And bubble of oil. Smog and sweet love! We had the music for the whale-
death of the world.   About us the environment crumbled

In yellow light.   There was no forth-
coming of wave-silver, but silver would flash now
And then through, turning side-on in many mullet
To the sun to die, as I tuned
The wild guitar. This won't get any worse
Until tomorrow, I said
Of Los Angeles, gazing out through "moderate eye
damage"   twisting the pegs   and under the strings

—The gray crane spanned his level, gracious flight

    Knowing better than to come
    To rest on anything, or touch
    Zuma Point here and now.

                  —O sea

    Of California, thou Pacific,
   For which the multitude of mortals bound
   Go trembling headlong and with terrific
   Outcry are drowned:
                 Day-moon meant more

Far from us   dazing the oil-slick with the untouched remainder
    Of the universe   spreading   contracting
       Catching fish at the living end
   In their last eye   the guitar rang moon and murder
And Appalachian love, and sent them shimmering from the cliff

    —The burning season shone
   On the vast feather-shapes of the open
     Sea tranquilized by off-
  shore drilling
       where gulls flapped in black   49

Gold   black
Magic of corporations—

—So here did mix the land's breath and the sea's:
Among the beautiful murders
Showering down ballad
After ballad on the rainbows of forever lost
Petroleum that blew its caps and turned on
All living things, we sang and prayed for purity, scattered everywhere
Among the stones
Of other worlds   and asked the moon to stay off us
As far as it always had, and especially far
From L.A.   I playing from childhood also
Like the Georgia mountains   the wind out of Malibu whipped her
Long hair into "Wildwood Flower"   her blue eye   *—whose eye*
Was somewhat strangely more than blue
Closed
                    —and if we lived
We were the cresting of a tide wherein
An endless motion rose exemplified.
                              In

—The gentle ecstasy of earth

And ruination, we lay on the threatened grass
Of cliffs, she tangled in my strings, her dark hair tuned
To me, the mountains humming back
Into resolution, in the great low-crying key
Of A.
                    —*I saw the moon and heard her sing.*
        I saw her sing and heard the moon.

            O vibrating mountains and bronze
    Strings, O oil-slicks in the moderately damaged eye
            And the sides of fish flashing out
One more time   birds black with corporations, turn me over to those

—*Maddened with hunger for another world:*
                                She lies in Glendale,
    In Forest Lawn.
                                O astronauts,
                Poets, all those
    Of the line of wizards and saviors, spend your lives
            And billions of dollars to show me
            The small true world
    Of death, the place we sang to
From Zuma. I read and imagine everything   51

I can of the gray airless ground
Of the moon   sphere cracked and bombarded
By negation   pure death, where death has not
Yet come
    —where yet no God appears:
                        Who knows?
There might be some unknown
Consolation in knowing California
Is not the deadest world of all
Until tomorrow: might be some satisfaction
Gone spatial   some hope
Like absolute zero, when the earth can become

    —The last of earthly things
Carelessly blooming in immensity
                and live men ride
Fleeing outward
    —a white flame tapering at the core of space   their hatches
    —Firm-barred against the fearful universe   until

    In the easy-leaping country
Of death, beings *—still armored in their visionary gold*
52   *Do human deeds.*

What deeds?
                              Will Los Angeles rise from the Sea
Of Tranquillity, on a great bubble
Of capped breath and oil?   Not yet;
The first men will see that desolation
Unimproved, before the freeways
Link it to Earth.   Ah, to leap or lie
On some universal ruin
Not ruined by us!   To be able to say—*Am I dead*
That I'm so far?
                              But where I stand,
Here, under the moon, the moon
—Breaks desperate magic on the world I know,

On Glendale.   *—All through the shadows crying grows, until*
The wailing is like grass upon the ground.
                                             It is I

Howling like a dog for the moon, for Zuma Point no matter what
The eye-damage   howling to bring her back note
By note like a childhood mountain
In the key of A   or, lacking that, howling
For anything   for the ultimate death   pure death

For the blaze of the outer dark   for escape
From L.A. smoldering and eye-
burning along the freeways   from rubber-smoke
And exhaust streaming *into the endless shadow*
Of my memory.   —*Let me grind alone*
And turn my knuckles in the granite
Of the moon
                              where underfoot the stones
—*wild with mysterious truth*
                                        lie in their universal
              Positions, in a place of no breath
And one machine
                              and for these reasons and many
Another I was quartered and drawn
To Cape Canaveral, with my tangled dream of Los Angeles
And death and the moon, my dead girl still tuned to me
In my tangled guitar.   The environment crumbled
              In red light, and raised up by dawn
Almighty buildings.
                              I felt a time-like tremor in my limbs.
              I wished to be bound that morning

For the true dead land, the land made to sustain
No life at all, giving out the unruined light
That shines on the fish-slicks of Zuma.
                    —*Are we the people of the end?*
                                        Before us all
                    The sun burst
From a machine   timed   slowly   tilting   leaning
    Upward   drawn moonward inch by inch   faster
        Faster   a great composite roar battered
                Like a board at the very bone
                Marrow, and in the hardshell case
            I sat on, the strings vibrated not with
    Mountains   but made the shapeless and very
                Music of the universal
        Abyss
                    —*and all the air*
            Was marvelous and sorrowful
                                    as we beheld,
    Exploding with solitude   blasting into the eyes and body,
            Rising   rising in dreadful machine-
pain as we prayed   as the newsmen fell to their knees   as the quality of life   55

And death changed forever
For better or worse
      —Apollo springing naked to the light.

      Nothing for me
Was solved. I wandered the beach
Mumbling to a dead poet
In the key of A, looking for the rainbow
Of oil, and the doomed
Among the fish.
      —Let us speak softly of living.

Head-Deep in Strange Sounds:
Free-Flight Improvisations
from the unEnglish

Purgation

—Po Chu-yi—

Beyond the eye, grasses go over the long fields.
Every season it happens, as though I—no; I and you,
Dear friend—decreed it. It is what we would like to have,

And it is there.
                          It is the season for wildfire,
And it will come, but will never quite get every one
Of the grasses. There is some green left, this year as last,

For us. Once more they are tall
In the April wind. They make the old road *be*

The road, where you and I go toward the old, beetle-eaten
City gate. Oh, fire, come *on!* I trust you.

My ancient human friend, you are dead, as we both know.

But I remember, and I feel the grass and the fire
Get together in April   with you and me, and that
Is what I want   both age-gazing living and dead

       both sighing like grass and fire.

The Ax-God: Sea-Pursuit

—after Alfred Jarry—

On the horizon, through the steam of exhausted blast-furnaces   fog   Yes
Pure Chance blows, as though it were really itself   blows
Not very well, and moans and shakes bells.

These are the sounds that invented salt.   But, listen,
Waves, we are among the arced demons you are hiding

In the visiting green gullies of your mountains.
Where the shoreline clamps a lost quivering over all
Of us, a huge and shadow-cast shape looms over muck.
We crawl round his feet, loose as lizards,

While, like a filthy Caesar on his chariot,
Or on a marble, leg-crossing plinth,
Carving a whale-boat from a tree-trunk, he . . .

Well, in that branching boat, he'll run
Us down, league for league   down   down to

The last of the sea's center-speeding
Center-spreading and ropeless knots. Green   blue   white
Time space distance: starting from the shore

His arms of unhealable, veined copper   over us
Raise to Heaven a breathing blue ax.

Nameless

(near Eugenio Montale)

Sure.   All the time I come up on the evil
$\qquad\qquad\qquad\qquad\qquad$ of just living:

It's been the strangled creek that still tries
To bubble like water   it's been the death-rattling leaf
Dried out for no reason
$\qquad\qquad\qquad\qquad$ and the tripped-sprawling horse.

As for anything good: you find it for me
And I'll look at it.   All I can come up with
Is an enclosure: the religion-faking sun-blasted rack
Of divine Indifference.   As I say, Sure:

It's the statue in its somnolescence
Of primitive, hectored stone.   It's noon

And cloud   and the falcon in circles,
Who planes, as high as he can get,

$\qquad\qquad$ For nothing.
$\qquad\qquad\qquad\qquad\qquad\qquad\qquad\qquad\qquad$ 63

Math

—Lautréamont—

Numbers who can't ever hear me
                  I'll say it anyway
All the way from my age-old school. You're still in my heart,
    And I can feel you go through there
Like a clean sea-wave. I breathed-in, instinctively,
From the one-two, one-two counts
    Of the soft-rocking cradle

    As drinking from a universal spring
                  older than the sun:

Numbers. There is this wave of matched, watched numbers
In my school-soul. Sometimes it is like smoke: I can't get through it.
Sometimes I believe that you've put   put in place of my heart
Inhuman logic.   Coldness
              beyond bearing. And yet . . . because of you

My intelligence has grown far beyond me
                                         from the frozen, radiant center
Of that ravishing clarity you give: give to those
      Who most truly love you   and can find you: *Listen*, ever-deaf numbers.
                                         Hail!   *I* hail you

             Arithmetic!   Algebra!   Geometry!

          Triangle gone luminous!

Judas

*—Georg Heym, resurrected from
under the ice—*

Mark.   Hair, one strand of it, can curl
Over your forehead like a branding-iron.
And meaningless winds   and many voices can be whispering
Like creek-flow, staying and going by.

But he runs close to His side like a mongrel,
And in the sick mud he picks up everything said
To him, and weighs it in his quivering hands.

                                           It is dead.

Ah, most gently in the swaying dusk,
The Lord walked down
Over the white fields.   Ear by ear, green by green,
Yellow by yellow, the corn-ears, the stalks, the sheer *growing*
Glorified. His feet were as small as houseflies, as they were perpetually being

Sent-down step by step
                    From the golden hysteria of Heaven.

Small Song

*—from the Hungarian of Attila Jozsef,
head crushed between two boxcars—*

I'm laughing, but being very quiet about it.
I've got my pipe and my knife:
I am quiet, and laughing like hell.

All hail, Wind! Let my song fall in jigsaw fragments!
Nobody is my friend except the one who can say
"I take pleasure in his misery."

I am of shadow and of sun   of the sun
          Returning always,

And I laugh, silently.

Undersea Fragment in Colons

—Vicente Aleixandre—

Swordfish, I know you are tired: tired out with the sharpness of your face:
    Exhausted with the impossibility of ever
Piercing the shade: with feeling the tunnel-breathing streamline of your flesh
    Enter and depart   depart
                        spirit-level after level of Death
            Tamped flat, and laid
Where there is no hillside grave.
                  Take this as it settles, then: word
    That behind your incomparable weapon chokes and builds,
      Blocked and balanced in your sides
        Instinct with meridians: word: the x-mark of certain world-numbers
        Blood-brothering   rising blade-headed
To an element as basic as the water
                unraveling in layers from around you:
      Strata trapped and stitched

By your face like tapestry
                              thinning   exploding
        The depth-imploded isinglass eye
                                    west of Greenwich and shocked
Into latitude   into the sea-birds' winged sea   tonnage of shifting silence now
                    Freed to the unleashed Time
        And timing of coordinates: all-solid light:

Pierceable sun   its flash-folded counterpart beneath
        By the billion: word: in one leap the layers,

        The slant ladder of soundlessness: word: world: sea:
            Flight partaking of tunnels   fins, of quills and airfoils:
            Word: unwitnessed numbers   nailed noon   enchanted three minutes
Of the sun's best effort of height   this space   time   this
            Hang-period   meridian passage:
                            Sing.

Mexican Valley

—homage and invention, Octavio Paz—

The day works on
        works out its transparent body. With fire, the bodiless hammer,
Light knocks me flat.
        Then lifts me.   Hooked on-
to the central flame-stone, I am nothing but a pause between
Two vibrations
        of pressureless glow: Heaven
And trees. Tlaloc help me
        I am pure space:
One of the principle future-lost battlefields
Of light. Through my body, I see my other bodies

Flocking and dancing   fighting each other
With solar joy. Every stone leaps inward, while the sun tears out my eyes
And my Heaven-knifed, stone-drunken heart.
        Yes,
70 But behind my gone sight is a spiral of wings.

                                        Now   *now*
My winged eyes are fetched-back and singing: yes singing like buzzards
            From the black-feathered crown-shifts of air
        Have always wished to be singing
                                    over this valley.
And I lean over my song
        Within trees, God knows where,
                                    in Mexico.
No matter what they say, it is not bad here. No, it is good:
It is better than anything the astronomers can dream up
With their sweaty computers. I've shaved my chest off to be
        Slowly-nearer and now without junk-hair
That is not really me   instantaneously nearer
        Soft universal power! It is warm, it is maybe even a little
Too hot, but glorious, here at the center   all the center there is
Before history . . . I send you a searing Yes
From the thousand cross-glittering black-holes of obsidian:
            I am like the *theory* of a blade
        That closes rather than opens   *closes*:
        That sends something back
Other than blood. Among leaves, I have torn out the heart of the sun

        The long-lost Mexican sun.

Low Voice, Out Loud

—Léon-Paul Fargue—

A good many times I've come down among you.
I've brought down my mountains, and washed them, just as a cloud would have done.
But you   YOU   cannot even begin to guess the *space*
Of the great shadows that've just gone past us.

But, look:

I come out of you!

I was your hands   your life-work
Your bleeding eyes   your red cubby-hole!   And that guitar:

To you, one touch of E minor is suicide!

I need you.

I have lifted the anchor.

For the thousandth time

I have smelled your shoes.

There I have done it, close to you and me:

I have lifted the anchor.

                         Whoever loves well

Punishes well.   But don't go

Against my rhythm.

                  It is by you that the man   in this case myself

Limits himself to being   his own being

A man: Identity blind, deaf

And indivisible!

                    I am tired of existing

As an animal of intelligence—

Don't try to name what is nameless.

Nothing. Everything. Nothing.

                     Rest easy, love. It is best:

Let us go back into the immense and soft-handed, double

Fire-bringing ignorance.

Poem

—from the Finnish of Saima Harmaja—

O death, so dear to me,
Do you remember when someone loved you?

Let all our blood-kin come back, into
Your soft, embalmed half-shadow.

Look.   I'm making no gestures.
I like and don't like
Your diligent work.   I try not to pay attention.
Other troubles I can stand.   Not yours.

Free my soul
                    and open your blinding jail.

O my sweet, owned death,
Lift the used-up one,
The soul half-opened as a wound

                                        and let him fly.

When

—Pierre Reverdy—

A prisoner in this space perpetually narrow
With my left-over hands left on my eyelids
With none of the words that reason can bring itself

To invent
                    I play the hell-game
That dances on the horizon. Space in darkness makes it better,

And it may be there are people passing through me—
There may even be a song
                              of some kind

        The cloud fills itself full of hovering holes

        The needle loses itself
        In clothes-covered sharpness

        The thunder stops short—

A few more minutes
                    I start to shake:
It's too late   too late ever to act   to act at all:

This is the thing as it will be.
All around, chains are gritting on each other
Like blackboard chalk   every tree
In the world is going to fall.

The window opens to summer.

A Saying of Farewell

—homage, Nordahl Grieg—

You've dressed yourself so white for it! And you poise
As on the edge of an undersea cliff, for departure.
We two are the only ones who know that this lost instant
        Is not lost, but is the end
           Of life.

"It's as though we were dying, this calm twilight."
  No; only you. I hang on watch,
High up in Time. Step off and fall as the wind rolls the earth

Over you like a wave. I am left on duty with the heart
    Going out over everything, no sleep

      In sight   braced,   monster-eyed,
Outstaring the shaken powder of fatigue   mist—
    By your clothes and mine white-bled

Raging with discovery like a prow
    Into the oncoming Never.

Three Poems with Yevtushenko

I. I Dreamed I Already Loved You

I dreamed I already loved you.
I dreamed I already killed you.

But you rose again; another form,
A girl on the little ball of the earth,
Naive simplicity, curve-necked
On that early canvas of Picasso,
And prayed to me with your ribs
"Love me," as though you said, "Don't push me off."

I'm that played out, grown-up acrobat,
Hunchbacked with senseless muscles,
Who knows that advice is a lie,
That sooner or later there's falling.

I'm too scared to say I love you
Because I'd be saying I'll kill you.

For in the depths of a face I can see through
I see the faces—can't count them—

Which, right on the spot, or maybe
Not right away, I tortured to death.

You're pale from the mortal balance.   You say
"I know everything;   I was all of them.
I know you've already loved me.
I know you've already killed me.
But I won't spin the globe backwards
We're on: Love again, and then kill again."

Lord, you're young.   Stop your globe.
I'm tired of killing.   I'm not a damn thing but old.

You move the earth beneath your little feet,
You fall, "Love me."
It's only in those eyes—so similar, you say
"This time don't kill me."

II. Assignation

No, no! Believe me!
                        I've come to the wrong place!
I've made a god-awful mistake! Even the glass
In my hand's an accident
                        and so's the gauze glance
Of the woman who runs the joint.
                              "Let's dance, huh?
You're pale . . .
                Didn't get enough sleep?"
And I feel like there's no place
To hide, but say, anyway, in a rush
"I'll go get dressed . . .
                   No, no . . . it's just
That I ended up out of bounds . . ."
And later, trailing me as I leave:
                     This is where booze gets
                           you . . .
What do you mean, 'not here'? *Right* here! Right here every time!
You bug everybody, and you're so satisfied

With yourself about it.   Zhenichka,
You've got a problem."
                              I shove the frost of my hands
Down my pockets, and the streets around are snow,
Deep snow.   I dive into a cab.   Buddy, kick this thing!   Behind
                                                         the Falcon
There's a room.   They're supposed to be waiting for me there.
She opens the door
                   but what the hell's wrong with her?
Why the crazy look?
                         "It's almost five o'clock.
You sure you couldn't come a little later?
Well, forget it.   Come on in.   Where else could you go now?"
Shall I explode
              with a laugh
                                or maybe with tears?
I tell you I was scribbling doggerel
                              but I got lost someplace.
I hide from the eyes.   Wavering I move backwards:
"No, no!   Believe me!   I've come to the wrong place!"
Once again the night
              once again snow

and somebody's insolent song
and somebody's clean, pure laughter.
I could do with a cigarette.
In the blizzard Pushkin's demons flash past
And their contemptuous, bucktoothed grin
Scares me to death.
                And the kiosks
And the drugstores
             and the social security offices
Scare me just as much . . .
                No, no! Believe me! I've ended up
In the wrong place again . . .
             It's *horrible* to live
And even more horrible
            not to live . . .
                  Ach, this being homeless
Like the Wandering Jew . . . Lord! Now I've gotten myself
Into the wrong century
           wrong epoch
                geologic era
                    wrong number

The wrong place again
                    I'm wrong
                              I've got it wrong . . .
I go, slouching my shoulders like I'd do
if I'd lost some bet,
                    and Ah, I know it . . . everybody knows it . . .
I can't pay off.

III.   Doing the Twist on Nails

When you throw your dancing shoes out, back over your shoulder,
And lose yourself, you find yourself twisting on the stage,
dancing,
dancing,
dancing—
let that pink boy whip you around—I can tell you:
Life doesn't dance this way—
That way dances death.
Thighs
shoulders
breasts:
they're all in it!
Inside you, dead drunk,
wheezes of air are dancing
Somebody else's ring
dances on your hand,
And your face by itself
doesn't dance at all
84   Flying, lifelessly, above all the body's life

Like a mask taken off your dead head.
And this stage—
                        is only one part of that cross
On which they once
                        crucified Jesus;
The nails shot through to the other side, and you began
To dance on them,
                        sticking out.
                                        And you dance

On the nails
                nails
On sandals red as rust
                        on the thorn-points of tears: Listen,
Because I once loved you, tiresomely, gloomily,
I also hammered the crooks of my nails
                                        into this page.

Ah, bestial, beastly music,
                        do you keep on getting stronger?
No one can see the blood
                        ooze from your foot-soles—
To wash the steps with clean water,
I'd rather you'd do it, Mary Magdalene,

                                        not Jesus.
I'll wash all their days, their yesterdays, not like a brother would
For a sister,
                        but like a sister for a sister.
I'll kneel down and pick up your feet
And hold them quietly, and with kisses try to do something
About their wounds.